21 POWERFUL AND PRACTICAL THINGS TO DO WHILE WAITING TO BE WED

Kadeen Dobbs

21 POWERFUL AND PRACTICAL THINGS TO DO WHILE WAITING TO BE WED. Copyright © 2021. **Kadeen Dobbs**. All Rights Reserved.

Printed in the United States of America.

No portion of this book may be reproduced, stored in a retrieval system, or transmitted in any form or by any means, except for brief quotations in printed reviews, without the prior written permission of DayeLight Publishers or **Kadeen Dobbs**.

ISBN: 978-1-953759-41-2 (paperback)

Scripture quotations marked "KJV" are taken from the Holy Bible, King James Version (Public Domain).

Scripture quotations marked (NLT) are taken from the Holy Bible, New Living Translation, copyright © 1996, 2004, 2007 by Tyndale House Foundation. Used by permission of Tyndale House Publishers, Inc., Carol Stream, Illinois 60188. All rights reserved.

Scripture quotations marked "ESV" are from the ESV Bible® (The Holy Bible, English Standard Version®), copyright © 2001 by Crossway Bibles, a publishing ministry of Good News Publishers. Used by permission. All rights reserved.

Scripture quotations marked "NKJV" are taken from the New King James Version. Copyright © 1982 by Thomas Nelson, Inc. Used by permission. All rights reserved. Bible text from the New King James Version® is not to be reproduced in copies or otherwise by any means except as permitted in writing by Thomas Nelson, Inc., Attn: Bible Rights and Permissions, P.O. Box 141000, Nashville, TN 37214-1000.

Scripture quotations marked (NIV) are taken from the Holy Bible, New International Version®, NIV®. Copyright © 1973, 1978, 1984 by Biblica, Inc.™ Used by permission of Zondervan. All rights reserved worldwide.

Affirmations For Singles

I am single but not lacking.
I am single but not desperate.
I am single, but not lonely,
I am single, but not inadequate.
I am single but not unhappy.
I am single but at peace with my situation.
I am single, but I am still God's beloved and the apple of His eye.
I am single but not deficient.
Being single is not a sickness
Or a life-threatening disease
It does not mean I will die alone
It just means God's best is on his/her way.

For single men and women. Pursue you!

Table of Contents

Affirmations For Singles 3
Preface 9
1   Build Your Relationship With Christ 15
2   Practicing Abstinence 27
3   Healing 33
4   Start A Business 41
5   Write A Book And Publish It 47
6   Educate Yourself 53
7   Find Another Stream Of Income 57
8   Read Books 63
9   Travel 67
10   Volunteer 73
11   Find A Cause That You Are Passionate About And Get Invested
.... 77
12   Learn A New Skill 83
13   Change Your Career 89
14   Get Healthier 93
15   Mend Broken Family Relationships 97

16	Learn A New Sport	101
17	Develop A Relationship With Yourself	103
18	Save: Get Your Finances In Order	111
19	Treat Yourself, In Moderation	113
20	Meditate On Gods Promises	115
21	Pray	119
22	His And Hers Prayer Book And Journal	123
	About The Author	127

Preface

Marriage is a desirable notion that must be built on the premise of God's divine timing. I do not know about you, but I would rather wait to be with my God-chosen spouse than let societal norms predicate that I must be wed by a certain age and, thus, have me engaged in a relationship that may ultimately lead to misery or divorce.

Indeed, a woman's role has transcended beyond the union of marriage. Women have become more liberated and proactive in their choices and, thus, are not pressured by the conventions placed on the periodic era to be wed. A woman's role has evolved and become more multi-faceted. It is no longer limited to being a spouse and motherhood. Marriage is not a must, but for most women, that want or preconceived need can consume their every waking hour. It becomes a sore that festers and oozes impatience, frustration, self-pity, woeful thoughts of impending and looming self-esteem issues and spinsterhood, feelings of envy, and enmity towards others because of their apparent wedding bliss.

From a societal perspective, a man's singlehood is deemed more attractive as he ages. Women may see it as a competition to be the female who wins his heart. Women appear to pursue marriage, whereas men seem to try to resist it. However, some men find the idea of marriage pleasant and want to meet that special one at the altar.

Nevertheless, holy matrimony is given by God. Holy matrimony is a blessing that is embedded and rooted on the very solid rock and foundation of Christ. Holy matrimony is a representation of a cord of three strands that cannot be easily broken: you, your spouse, and the Holy Spirit. Holy matrimony embodies two standing as one and resisting the fiery darts of the enemy and so are not easily overpowered. Holy matrimony is the epitome of a sanctified and consecrated union for the purpose of advancing, working for, or bettering God's kingdom.

I, therefore, want more than a marriage. I want holy matrimony, and this is worth waiting for because, as for this woman, not just any man will do. The only man for me is who God has preordained for me.

Factors that may determine or influence a man and woman to desire marriage are:

1. Their relationship with Jesus Christ
2. Their family background
3. Age
4. Culture
5. Loneliness
6. Past relationship/s
7. Family pressure/expectations
8. Friendships/peers
9. A desire for children in a marital home
10. To feel loved and secure
11. To socialize

12. To have sex within the context of marriage

There are so many other reasons that may be less than chivalrous and beautiful for an individual to hope for marriage, but as a child of God, you can stand on this:

"If you then, who are evil, know how to give good gifts to your children, how much more will your Father who is in heaven give good things to those who ask him!" (Matthew 7:11 – ESV).

What is the above scripture stating as a fact?

ASK for what you need.

Ask Who? Your Heavenly Father (God).
Ask for what? Anything.
Anything? Yes, anything.

Ask God for a good husband or wife with all the qualities you desire and ask that HIS will be done in the matter. God knows what is best for you. He created your spouse.

Not all women and men, however, will marry, nor do they want to. But while in waiting for your spouse, must everything be drab and monotonous? Must life be uneventful and less than charming? Can one not better him or herself while waiting?

You may be asking yourself, *"Why am I not yet married? Why have I not yet met the one? Why has he/she not found me? Does God not love me? Why do I always fall for the wrong person? Am I not beautiful enough or handsome enough or successful enough? Why do I attract the types that I am not attracted to or see myself spending the rest of my life with?"* Stop torturing yourself right this instant! Enough with the self-analytical internal interrogation; it is mental abuse.

A wait seems less lengthy when one is not simply preoccupied but enjoying oneself.

The overused cliché "time flies when one is having fun" is applicable here. However, I will add a tad more. Fun is not necessarily defined or labeled as having fun out in the club, drinking till the wee hours of the morning, engaging in reckless once-in-a-lifetime adventures, becoming involved in forgettable, meaningless, and numerous relationships just to pass the time. Rather, when you wait patiently, you gain perspective, self-worth, and wisdom. You fall in love with yourself and become even more prepared for the man or woman God created for you. Your outlook on life becomes positive, optimistic, and you think less about when you will meet that special one and more on developing yourself spiritually, intellectually, emotionally, socially, and physically. The road to self-discovery can be blissfully surprising, wonderful, and filled with experiences that can be captured and framed in the mind's eye, on blank pages, on a video, and in a photograph. As you become invested in getting to know yourself, you increase the inevitable possibility of uncovering YOUR PURPOSE.

This is why I have compiled and written in this book a list of things a man and woman can do while waiting to be proposed to or waiting to propose and experience holy matrimony.

Do not get busy simply to pass the time. Get engaged. Get involved. Get immersed. Get engrossed. Become industrious in developing YOU and finding YOUR PURPOSE!

1
Build Your Relationship With Christ

You do not truly know where you are going until you have found Jesus, and when you do, where you are headed will not really matter because you have found Jesus. God will never lead you down a path of destruction because He gives only good gifts to His children.

The road to God is through Jesus, and your faith gives you HOPE in a future that was planned by the most high God, your Creator.

Here are some things to expect when you focus on building your relationship with God and not on marriage:

1. Acceptance of your current single situation, which equates to peace with where you are at in life and not forcing things to change but rather waiting on God to change them for you as you seek Him.

2. An inner feeling of contentment which bubbles over into joy. Joy is intrinsic. It is a deep-seated feeling that erupts in laughter and finding pleasure in the most mundane and simple things. It is waking up alone, yet still feeling happy. It is sipping tea on a rainy day at home, realizing there is no one sharing a "cuppa"(cup of tea) with you, yet still feeling

content. It is dining at a restaurant alone and seeing a married couple being in love, and you stare, not with envy but with love.

3. When one is waiting for God's best, nothing less will do, so self-control is practiced without effort. The desire to settle becomes obsolete. How can you settle for a fling? How can a one-night stand ever satisfy? How can an uncertain entry and exit into a relationship do when God has greater plans for you? Self-control is easier when sex is not perceived only as sexual gratification but something to be enjoyed in the context of marriage. Sex will not be the primary desire; instead, NOT fornicating will be.

4. There is a difference between waiting and waiting patiently. To wait is to think about something constantly; you are eager for it to happen, so it is never too far from your forethoughts, no matter how busy you get. However, when you wait patiently, you not only tolerate delays, but you remain composed, serene, purposeful, and positive during this time of being found and waiting to find the one who complements your purpose. Your purpose will marry too, so your partner must align with what God has put you here to fulfill; all the more reason to wait on God's perfect timing.

5. A manifestation of the fruit of the Spirit will become more prominent as it relates to how you handle and approach situations. Maturity will blossom from the inner man, so one's intellectual and emotional capacity extends to a level where scenarios are handled from a more Christ-like perspective and not the physical, immediate self that reacts without thought. You will become filled with the fruit of the Spirit and experience inner joy, peace, compassion, love,

patience, self-control, gentleness, faith, modesty, and forbearance during trials and tribulations. These qualities will equip you to handle life, relationships, and make you a better spouse and, most importantly, a person one can live with.

Living with someone is an enormous step. This is inevitable after marriage. Your union is complete after you begin to share a bed and become one flesh. You begin to look like the person you spend the most time with, not just externally, but internally. As your lives merge, so does your personality, ways, and attitudes, both good and bad. Ensure that what you give off to your spouse: the energy, atmosphere, attributes, characteristics, idiosyncrasies, and habitual practices are what you would like to receive because who you are on the inside will be reflected in how your spouse acts. We are not perfect human beings, but we can become a better version of our current self.

Biblical affirmations you can say daily as you wait for your Godly spouse (for women):

1. I am seeking the kingdom of God first and His righteousness so everything I need in a husband will be given to me, for it is written in Matthew 6:33: "But seek first the kingdom of God, and his righteousness; and all these things will be added unto you." (ESV).

2. I am submitted to my future husband because I understand and accept that he is the head of the household, for it is written in Ephesians 5:22-24: "Wives, submit to your own husbands, as to the Lord. For the husband is the head of the wife, even as Christ is the head of the church: his body and

is himself its Saviour. Therefore, as the church submits to Christ, so also wives should submit in everything to their husbands." (ESV).

3. I am a wise and understanding wife to my future husband, for it is written in Proverbs 19:14: "House and wealth are inherited from fathers, but a prudent wife is from the Lord." (ESV).

4. I am committed and faithful to my future husband, and he is to me, for it is written in Hebrews 13:4: "Let marriage be held in honour among all and let the marriage bed be undefiled for God will judge the sexually immoral and adulterous." (ESV).

5. I am working with my future husband and, as such, will receive a double portion for our combined efforts, for it is written in Ecclesiastes 4:9: "Two are better than one because they have a good reward for their toil." (ESV).

6. I am not afraid to love my future husband unconditionally for there is no fear in a love that has been approved by God, for it is written in 1 John 4:18: "There is no fear in love because perfect love casts out fear for fear has to do with punishment and whoever fears has not been perfected in love." (ESV).

7. I am trustworthy to my future husband. I will do good to him and for him and not harm him all the days of my life, for it is written in Proverbs 31:11-12: "The heart of her husband trusts in her and he will have no lack of gain. She does him good and not harm all the days of her life." (ESV).

8. I am a dignified wife who does not gossip and is treated with respect by her husband and possesses self-control and is trustworthy in all things, for it is written in 1 Timothy 3:11: "Their wives likewise must be dignified not slanderous but sober minded and is faithful in all things." (ESV).

9. I am honouring my future husband with humility, gentleness, patience, and with an eagerness to guard and keep the harmony and oneness produced in the spirit in the binding power of peace in our household, for it is written in Ephesians 4:2-3: "With all humility and gentleness with patience bearing one another in love eager to maintain the unity of the spirit in the bond of peace." (ESV).

10. I am unafraid to apologize to my future husband as he will be to me if either of us is in the wrong for the sun must not set nor must we retire together or sleep in a bed full of wrath and malice, for it is written in Ephesians 4:26: "Be angry and do not sin. Do not let the sun go down on your anger." (ESV).

11. I am delighting myself in the Lord, committing to Him and trusting Him to choose a husband who will not just meet and exceed the desires of my heart, for it is written in Psalm 37:4-5: "Delight yourself in the Lord and he will give you the desires of your heart. Commit your way to the Lord. Trust in him and he will act." (ESV).

12. I am the perfect complement to my future husband, for it is written in Genesis 2:18: "Then the Lord God said," It is not good that the man should be alone. I will make him a helper fit for him." (ESV).

13. I am an excellent wife to my future husband. To him I will be far more precious than jewels, for it is written in Proverbs 31:10: "An excellent wife who can find? She is far more precious than jewels." (ESV).

14. I am receiving whatever I have asked the Lord for in prayer concerning my future husband, and I have faith that I have received it, for it is written in Mark 11:24: "Therefore I tell you, whatever you ask in prayer, believe that you have received it, and it will be yours." (ESV).

15. I am in full awareness that the head of a woman is her husband and the head of my future household is Christ Jesus, for it is written 1 Corinthians 11:3: "But I want you to understand that the head of every man is Christ and the head of a wife is her husband, and the head of Christ is God." (ESV).

16. I am the beloved of my future husband, and I am his, for it is written in the book of Solomon 2:16a: "My beloved is mine and I am His." (ESV).

17. I am loving my future husband, and he will love me with an endless love that is patient, kind, without envy, arrogance, rudeness, and insistence on one's own way, for it is written in 1 Corinthians 13:4 : "Love is patient and kind. Love does not envy or boast. It is not arrogant or rude, does not insist on its own way, not irritable or resentful." (ESV).

18. I forgive anyone who may have hurt me in a past relationship, so my heart is free and open to love my future husband without bitterness, rage, and undeserved suspicion and judgment, for it is written in Ephesians 4:31-32: "Get rid of all bitterness, rage and anger, brawling and slander

along with every form of malice. Be kind and compassionate to one another forgiving just as in Christ, God forgave you." (NIV).

Let Us Pray

Our Father who art in heaven, hallowed be Thy name, Thy kingdom come, Thy WILL be done on earth. Thy WILL be done in my life as it is in heaven. Give us this day our daily bread and forgive us our debts as we forgive our debtors. Lead us not into temptation, but deliver us from the evil one, for Thine is the kingdom and the power and the glory, forever and ever. AMEN.

You will be faithful to your future husband, as he will be to you. Your marriage will be blessed and covered by the blood of Jesus. Your future husband will be chosen by God. You will be your husband's confidant and will not gossip about him with your friends or family. You will not seek the attention and affection of another male if you have an argument with your future husband. You will seek to rectify any problems that arise about him, with him. You will not withhold intimacy from your husband out of spite as you understand that this makes you manipulative. You will not be a quarrelsome wife, for it is written in Proverbs 21:9: "It is better to live in the corner of a housetop than in a house shared with a quarrelsome wife." (ESV). You are loving. You are supportive. You are affectionate. You listen. You offer advice, and you are intentional about spending time with your future husband. You show appreciation for the things he does to make you happy.

You will not share a bed with your future husband in anger but resolve every issue before you both fall asleep. You will pray together and pray for each other. You will read and study the Word of God together. You will tell him you love him, and you feel honoured to be his wife. You are the answer to a man's prayer; wait on God's perfect timing.

Ladies, if you prefer to listen to the audio version of these affirmations, they are available on my YouTube Channel @Kadeen Dobbs. Here is the link:
https://www.youtube.com/watch?v=1qKDJ31478w

Biblical affirmations you can say daily as you wait for your Godly spouse (for men):

1. I am seeking the kingdom of God first and His righteousness, so everything I need in a wife will be given to me, for it is written in Matthew 6:33: "But seek first the kingdom of God and his righteousness, and all these things will be added to you." (ESV).

2. I am loving my future wife with humility, and gentleness, with patience, bearing with her in love, eager to maintain the unity of the Spirit in the bond of peace in our household and marriage, for it is written in Ephesians 4:2-3: "With all humility and gentleness, with patience, bearing with one another in love, eager to maintain the unity of the Spirit in the bond of peace." (ESV).

3. I am loving my wife as Christ loves the church, for it is written in Ephesians 5:25: "For husbands, this means love your wives, just as Christ loved the church. He gave up his life for her." (NLT).

4. I am committed to my future wife, for it is written in Mark 10:9: "Therefore what God has joined together, let no one separate." (NIV).
5. I am doing everything with my future wife in LOVE, for it is written in 1 Corinthians 16:14: "Do everything in love." (NIV).

6. I am loving my wife deeply and will treat her with respect, for it is written in Ephesians 5:28: "So ought men to love their wives as their own bodies. He that loveth his wife loveth himself." (KJV).

7. I am the husband of a virtuous woman, for it is written in Proverbs 31:10: "Who can find a virtuous woman? For her prize is far above rubies." (KJV).

8. I am speaking to my wife with respect and will therefore respond accordingly even when angry, for it is written in Proverbs 15:1: "A soft answer turneth away wrath: but grievous words stir up anger." (KJV).

9. I am blessed with a good wife from the Lord, for it is written in Proverbs 19:14: "House and riches are the inheritance of fathers: and a prudent wife is from the Lord." (KJV).

10. I am living joyfully with my wife, all the days of my life on this earth, for it is written in Ecclesiastes 9:9: "Live joyfully with the wife whom thou lovest all the days of the life of thy vanity, which he hath given thee under the sun, all the days of thy vanity; for that is thy portion in this life, and in thy labour which thou takest under the sun." (KJV).

11. I am committed to my lifelong partner, and I will stay with her till I die, for it is written in 1 Corinthians 7:10-11: "And unto the married, I command, yet not I, but the Lord, let not the wife depart from her husband; but and if she depart, let her remain unmarried or be reconciled to her husband: and let not the husband put away his wife." (KJV).

12. I am not going to bed angry with my wife, for it is written in Ephesians 4:26: "Be ye angry and sin not: let not the sun go down upon your wrath." (KJV).

13. I am faithful to my future wife as she will be to me, for it is written in Hebrews 13:4: "Marriage should be honoured by all and the marriage bed kept pure, for God will judge the adulterer and all the sexually immoral." (NIV).

14. I am loving my wife with patience, kindness, without dishonor, self-seeking, boastfulness, pride, envy, easily angered, and keeping a record of all wrongs. My love for her will always protect, trust, hope, and persevere, for it is written in 1 Corinthians 13:4-7: "Love is patient, love is kind. It does not envy. It does not boast, it is not proud. It does not dishonor others, it is not self-seeking, it is not easily angered; it keeps no record of wrongs. Love does not delight in evil but rejoices with the truth. It always protects, always trusts, always hopes, and always perseveres." (NIV).

Let Us Pray

Our Father who art in Heaven, hallowed be Thy name, Thy kingdom come, Thy WILL be done on earth. Thy will be done in my life as it is in heaven. Give us this day our daily bread and forgive us our debts as we forgive our debtors. Lead us not into temptation but deliver us from the evil one; for Thine is the kingdom and the power and the glory forever and ever. AMEN.

You will be faithful to your future wife, as she will be to you. Your marriage will be blessed and covered by the blood of Jesus. Your future wife will be chosen by God. You will be your wife's confidant and will not gossip about her with your friends or family. You will not seek the attention and affection of another female if you have an argument with your future wife. You will seek to rectify any problems that arise about her, with her. You will not withhold intimacy from your wife out of spite, as you understand that this makes you manipulative. You will not be a quarrelsome husband, for it is written in Luke 6:31: *"And as you wish that others would do to you, do so to them." (ESV).*

You are loving. You are supportive. You are affectionate. You listen. You offer advice, and you are intentional about spending time with your future wife. You show appreciation for the things that she does to make you happy. You will not share a bed with your future wife in anger but resolve every issue before you both fall asleep. You will pray together and pray for each other. You will read and study the Word of God together. You will tell her that you love her, and you feel honoured to be her husband. You are the answer to a woman's prayer; wait on God's perfect timing.

2
Practicing Abstinence

A person who chooses abstinence is one who has decided to abstain or stay away from sexual intercourse. This also means no masturbation or use of sexual toys. Society has become more liberal about sexual gratification and freedom. However, while you are waiting to wed, it is a wonderful time to wait for God's best. It is, therefore, a great time not to be watching or reading content that will sexually arouse you. In addition, the closer you get to God, the less you will desire to see certain content. It loses its appeal if it once did.

Reasons To Practice Abstinence

- To spare yourself a heartbreak.

There are men and women who have sex without sexual entanglement. They view sex as a physical release, and that is it. They do not get attached emotionally. They see someone they desire, they pursue, get what they want and move on. Because you desire to get married, you begin a relationship at a place of vulnerability. You go in, hoping it will lead to a proposal. If you want to get married, why keep having sex with individuals who do not? If you want to get married, why not seek God's guidance in the matter so that you will meet who the Creator created for you? Why do you deliberately have to kiss many frogs before you find your prince or princess?

- To decrease contracting AIDS and STIs.

Sexually transmitted diseases are on the rise. AIDS rose rapidly in the 1980s, and there are approximately 38 million people and rising who are currently living in the world with it. There is still no cure, and the fact that it is increasing is an indication that many individuals do not practice safe sex. When you meet that special someone, there is time, as you get to know each other, to do blood work and check out each other's health status. If you plan to have children with someone, it is great to know what may run in their family genetically. Is there sickle anemia? Diabetes? Heart conditions? What is their blood type? Are you both compatible on paper as it relates to your DNA make-up? If you have children together, will there be birth defects?

Viruses, such as herpes, human papillomavirus, and hepatitis are also incurable. If you have any of these, you must disclose it to anyone who wants to marry you before marriage and sex. However, not everyone will inform you of their health issues, hence, wait. Lust, rushed sex, and unprotected sex can lead to irreversible, lifetime, detrimental consequences.

- Unprepared motherhood and fatherhood.

Children are gifts from God, but if they come when you are not ready financially, emotionally, and spiritually, you may raise a child with resentment and not enough love and resources to make them flourish and be effective and productive citizens of this world.

Reasons To Practice Abstinence From A Biblical Perspective

Even if you are not a virgin, it is not too late to abstain from sex. When you know better, you change and just not do certain things anymore, especially when you realize that your body is the temple of the Holy Spirit.

1 Corinthians 7:8-9: "To the unmarried and the widows I say that it is good for them to remain single, as I am. But if they cannot exercise self-control, they should marry. For it is better to marry than to burn with passion." (ESV).

Paul is stating that self-control should be practiced as a single person and that it is actually a good thing to remain single. In 1 Corinthians 7:34, it reads: "An unmarried woman or virgin is concerned with the Lord's affairs. Her aim is to be devoted to the Lord in body and spirit." (NIV). This is also applicable to a man. A single person is not preoccupied with finding "The One" but rather doing God's work and keeping their bodies sanctified. However, if one finds it difficult to control his/her sexual needs, then marry.

1 Corinthians 7:2: "But because of the temptation to sexual immorality, each man should have his own wife and each woman her own husband." (ESV).

God created sex. He created it as a pleasurable activity that should be enjoyed within the context of marriage because He knew that sex outside of marriage could lead to adultery, cheating on a respective partner, lusting, children growing up without a mother or father, and just fulfilling the flesh in a manner that would lead to spiritual and emotional deprivation, death and contracting a sexually transmitted disease.

Hebrews 13:4: "Let marriage be held in honor among all, and let the marriage bed be undefiled, for God will judge the sexually immoral and adulterous." (ESV).

Sex is beautiful, but sex within marriage equates to freedom. When you wait on God to choose your spouse, you will engage in sexual intercourse with someone you know you can TRUST. The fragility of that word "trust" is like cotton candy: sweet to the taste but too much and you experience tooth decay. Oh, how sweet it is to believe you can trust someone, but that emotion or action should not be easily given or reciprocated. You can trust yourself, but can you trust others?

Waiting on the one who God has chosen for you will increase and guarantee that your marital bed will be one that experiences fidelity. You will never have to worry that another will share your husband's or wife's bed and body.

Galatians 5:19-21: "Now the works of the flesh are evident: sexual immorality, impurity, sensuality, idolatry, sorcery, enmity, strife, jealousy, fits of anger, rivalries, dissensions, divisions, envy, drunkenness, orgies, and things like these. I warn you, as I warned you before, that those who do such things will not inherit the kingdom of God." (ESV).

Colossians 3:5: "Put to death, therefore, whatever belongs to your earthly nature: sexual immorality, impurity, lust, evil desires and greed, which is idolatry." (NIV).

If you focus on fulfilling the flesh, then sexual gratification has become an idol. An idol is something that you worship. What you worship is your god, hence, idolatry, which is a sin because one of the commandments is: "Thou shalt have no other gods before me." (Exodus 20:3 – (KJV). Please notice how the one true and living God begins with an uppercase or capital letter, and the other gods begin with a common or lowercase letter. Is this a mere coincidence? I believe not. My God is a big GOD who is not common. There is only one like HIM.

When sex is thought about constantly, it consumes the mind until a sex addiction occurs. Individuals may become nymphomaniacs, sadists and begin to engage in orgies and watching pornographic content. Sensuality, sexuality, and nude bodies are glorified in the 21st century, but as a man or woman, there is so much more to you than being a sexual being. What are your interests outside of the bedroom? Do not focus on your private organs. They are not just for sexual liaisons.

1 Corinthians 6:18-20: "Flee from sexual immorality. Every other sin a person commits is outside the body, but the sexually immoral person sins against his own body. Or do you not know that your body is a temple of the Holy Spirit within you, whom you have from God? You are not your own, for you were bought with a price. So glorify God in your body." (ESV).

You hurt your own body when you engage in sex outside of the context of marriage. You hurt yourself on the inside. Your body is the temple of God, so you hinder the Holy Spirit, the presence of God, to help you grow spiritually and love things not of the flesh or the world, but of God. You will have no desire to please God without the help of the Holy Spirit. Your body must be used to glorify God. Jesus paid the price on the cross for our sinful bodies.

Do not deliberately use it to engage in sexual immorality. You belong to God, even when you marry.

3
Healing

No matter how liberal and democratic the world becomes, a woman, even if she does not want to marry, is expected to have a diamond on her left ring finger. Believe me, this is the same for men. They also feel the pressure to marry. However, never let societal expectations make you rush into a commitment as serious as marriage.

The 21st century flaunts sexual exploration, multiple partners, and infidelity. I believe though that women cannot do what men do and still be considered a lady. Many may disagree, but my stance comes not just from worldly perceptions but from a biblical standpoint, which is why I will add this: a man is not truly a gentleman if he deliberately breaks the heart of a woman and deliberately pursues her when he knows he has no intention of marrying her, especially when she is vocal about wanting marriage and he pretends to reciprocate this desire. She has an outcome that varies from his mindset and, hence, it is like two parallel lines that appear to be going in the same direction, but will never meet; heartbreak is inevitable and the collision will leave only one severely damaged; the one who thought this would lead to the altar. Honesty is always and still is the best policy.

Genesis 2:24-25 reads: *"Therefore a man shall leave his father and his mother and hold fast to his wife, and they shall become one flesh. And the man and his wife were both naked and were not ashamed."* (ESV).

According to the scripture, when you have sexual intercourse with someone, you become one flesh. You intertwine with a man or woman and become one. That means you become one with everyone you have sex with. That means you bonded with someone other than your wife or husband, not just on a physical level, but on an emotional and spiritual level. No wonder when a relationship ends, you still feel attached. You exchange blood, saliva, and sweat when you mate.

Your skin is the largest organ. It receives stimuli from the outward world. Every sensation is felt because of the brain, and your brain remembers emotions and feelings, pleasant or unpleasant, because of nerve cells that connect called synapses. So, essentially, each time you try to get over or forget someone, your synapses give you a synopsis or addendum of who you left or who left you and all the emotions they evoked. That means many men and women are walking around with bits and pieces of their past lover because they engaged in another relationship while on the rebound or before healing properly.

The English Language is very interesting and literal. Did you know that the prefix 're' means again? So, this is something to ponder. When you enter a relationship while on the rebound, you are hurting yourself again. Rebound relationships are a diversion; they are a distraction and a hindrance to your healing process.

What does healing look or feel like?

- Thinking about that individual without bitterness and resentment, but rather with forgiveness and acceptance.

- Realizing that a past relationship has taught you about yourself by showing you what you will not accept or tolerate in another relationship and the qualities you really desire in your future spouse.

- When you no longer miss that person or crave their touch or need to hear their voice.

- When seeing him or her with someone else does not prick like a sharp needle in the heart. If it still does, you are human. Wounds take time to heal.

- When you wish him/her the best and mean it.

- When you can converse without ending up in bed. The relationship has ended. Stop having sex. You are strengthening sexual ties that need to be loosed/broken.

- When you can speak with civility to each other. If you cut all ties with someone and no longer speak to them or with them, it does not mean you are not healing. Every relationship ends differently and for various reasons.

- If you are not tempted to call or reach out just to hear their voice.

- When you no longer feel the desire to call him or her to tell him/her about your day, complain about an issue in your life, or seek comfort from him/her.

- You can do something alone that you used to love doing with your partner without being sad, angry, dissolving into tears, or avoid doing altogether.

- You no longer HATE him/her. You now feel peace. You feel Philia love (platonic friendship) for him or her and no longer Eros love (erotic and passionate).

Scriptures To Help You Heal

I believe the word of God is therapeutic because it is alive. Here is list of a few scriptures that you may read daily or often.

Jeremiah 29:11: "'For I know the plans I have for you,' declares the Lord, 'plans to prosper you and not to harm you, plans to give you hope and a future.'" (NIV).

Matthew 11:28: "Come to me, all you who are weary and burdened, and I will give you rest." (NIV).

Psalm 147:3: "He heals the brokenhearted and binds up their wounds." (ESV).

John 14:27: "Peace I leave with you; my peace I give you. I do not give it to you as the world gives. Do not let your hearts be troubled and do not be afraid." (NIV).

Romans 8:28: "And we know that for those who love God all things work together for good, for those who are called according to his purpose." (ESV).

Isaiah 43:18: "Forget the former things; do not dwell on the past." (NIV).

Isaiah 41:10: "So do not fear, for I am with you; do not be dismayed, for I am your God. I will strengthen you, I will help you; I will uphold you with my righteous hand." (NIV).

Psalm 34:18: "The Lord is close to the brokenhearted and saves those who are crushed in spirit." (NIV).

Psalm 30:5: "Weeping may stay for the night, but rejoicing comes in the morning." (NIV).

Psalm 55:22: "Cast your burden on the Lord, and He will sustain you; he will never permit the righteous to be moved." (ESV).

Philippians 4:6-7: "Do not be anxious about anything, but in every situation, by prayer and petition, with thanksgiving, present your requests to God. And the peace of God, which transcends all understanding, will guard your hearts and your minds in Christ Jesus." (NIV).

Do not relive; instead, release.

Here is a poem from my upcoming poetry book:

> DO NOT RELIVE, RELEASE
> Here you are stuck in the past
> Feeling so downcast
> Because the pain cut so deep.
>
> How could he do this to me?
> How could he hurt me so?
> How could he betray me like this?
> Did he not say he loved me?
> What did I do wrong?
> Was I not attentive enough?
> Did I not do enough?
> Didn't I dress right?
> Didn't I stick by him?
> Through thick and thin?
> Went out on a limb
> To show him I am in
>
> But to you I say,
> Let your past
> Be transformed
> By that Man from Galilee
> Who inflicts no hurts, gives no sorrow,
> Forgets all wrongs and will never forsake or leave you.
> Closer than a mother, father, sister, brother… and the one who betrayed you.
>
> If you trust this Man,
> He will give you the plan

To rise above the hurt, the pain, the betrayal.
With Him,
There will never be an "end."
He will give you a "new lease" on life,
So you can completely RE-LEASE!

This poem is applicable also to men, for they have experienced heartbreak as well. They have been hurt, betrayed, and extended genuine love to the wrong person, but the same ONE who can heal the broken heart of a man or woman is Jesus.

As you are healing, take the time as well to heal from issues that stem from your parentage. Heal from parental abandonment, neglect, the feeling of never being good enough, of being compared to your siblings, and always falling short in your family's eyes. Heal from the lack of love that your parents never gave. Heal from the betrayal of friends who stole your ideas at work and passed them off as their own; heal from being lied on and gossiped about and heal from the one who had a relationship with your partner behind your back. Let go mentally of business partners who left you in debt, stole your money, and left you bankrupt. Heal from having had to endure a rough childhood and living in foster homes, and holding down three jobs to make ends meet. Heal from the people who hurt you at church—the last place you would expect such an occurrence. Heal from that miscarriage. It was not your fault! Heal from being overlooked in that workplace for that promotion. God has better; that is the truth. Heal from that occurrence on the playground years ago that left you scarred or the bullying you endured in school. Heal from never being chosen to be a part of a team or always being the last to be picked. Heal from that one mistake that got you incarcerated or received a DUI. Heal from hurting someone you had no intention of doing wrong. Let it go!

Heal from whatever has hurt you, and when you ponder about it, there is anger and regret or a flood of negative emotions that just disrupts your mind, pricks your heart, and unsettles your soul. Now is the time to set things right within yourself for your release and breakthrough.

4
Start A Business

One of the best things you can do while waiting to be wed is starting a business. I know it is easier said than done because being an entrepreneur requires money, determination, persistence, hard work, long hours, sacrifices, and budgeting. However, what are the advantages of starting your own business?

- Your spouse will find you engaged in your God-given purpose.

God created you on purpose, with a purpose, and for a purpose, and while pursuing your purpose through your business endeavour, you will not be so engrossed with the fact that as a man, you have not yet found your wife, or as a woman, your husband has not yet found you. When it comes to starting a business, the rewards you envision may not be immediate, but sticking and working at it will reap successes beyond the now and for the future. A business-like marriage is a long-term investment that becomes more fulfilling as the years go by if you lay the right foundation and stick to it, for better or for worse. Let me hasten to add, be wise to know when to draw a new business plan and be even wiser when it comes to committing to another individual. A new business plan is easier to be redrafted than a husband or wife.

- Being your own boss.

When you own and operate a business of your own, the only BOSS you answer and are accountable to is God. Your focus will be on having your business thrive through different marketing techniques and strategies and not on your singlehood. You will be more invested because this is your business, effort, time, and money. Leadership qualities and skills will grow and make you a better spouse. However, women, remember the man's job is to lead. The Bible explicitly states this in 1 Corinthians 11:3: *"But I want you to understand that the head of every man is Christ, the head of a wife is her husband, and the head of Christ is God." (ESV).*

Women, do not be bossy and misinterpret this as leading and, therefore, belittle and emasculate your spouse. Wives can lead while serving. Husbands can lead without controlling. Find that balance.

- Clock in and out based on your schedule.

Your hours of working will be more flexible so you can pursue YOU! What does "pursuing you" look like? Doing things that enhance your self-worth and expanding your intellectual capacity and language, such as saying affirmations daily from the Word of God, eliminating friendships or conversations that devalue your self-esteem, exercising (you do not have to join a gym to exercise or get fit. You are about to start a business, so save not spend), eating better, conversing with positive people and other entrepreneurs, attending business workshops, financial workshops, and finding companies or individuals that give start-up cash to first-time business owners. Pursue you!

One's financial situation can always improve, and one way of doing that is by striving to become more financially independent. Here are some things to do/consider **before** opening your business:

1. Research your business idea.

    - Is there a demand for your service/product?
    - Will the demand for your product depreciate or increase over time?
    - Who is your audience or target group?
    - What is the ideal location for your business?
    - What is the start-up cost?
    - How will you finance it? Everybody's financial situation is different; you decide. If you are uncertain how to proceed, seek the advice of an expert.
    - How many members will you need for your staff? Can you singlehandedly do everything?
    - How much can you offer as a salary to prospective employees?

2. Do a business plan.

Set some SMART goals:

> **S**pecific
> **M**easurable
> **A**chievable
> **R**ealistic
> **T**ime based

As it relates to your business plan, whatever you choose to do, pace yourself. As the popular adage purports, "Rome wasn't built in a day" so theoretically, neither will your business. However, with goals in place, you will have a better idea where to place your focus and how to make effective decisions.

Think about the following:

- Where do you see your business in twelve months? Whatever your vision is, what steps will you put in place to ensure it occurs?

- What steps will you take to ensure that customer service is professional and excellent so your clientele grows?

- What measures will you put in place to satisfy your employee/s?

- How will you ensure that you stay ahead of the competition?

3. Marketing Your Business

Things you may do/consider to bring awareness to your product/service so it sells:

- Get a website to showcase products or services.

- Email marketing: Letting people know about what you are offering/selling via email.

You can start a blog to get more emails and expand your clientele. You can start a blog for free through Wix, WordPress, Weebly, Blogger, just to name a few. I have a blog that speaks about a plethora of spiritual topics at:
https://kadeendobbs.wixsite.com/soaringtomynewbeginn.
I started this for free through Wix.

- Advertising through various social platforms, for example, Instagram, Facebook, Twitter, WhatsApp, Zoom, and Tik Tok.

- Do flyers and business cards, and invest in advertisements.

- Reach out to radio stations, television networks, podcasts, or newspaper companies to talk about your product/service and, thus, doing interviews.

5
Write A Book And Publish It

Writing a book may seem very daunting. *Where do I begin? What do I write about? Will anyone purchase something I have written? Will they like it? When will I ever finish?*

I am encouraging you; I am imploring you, men and women, just START.

If you are not aware, my first book was *"Men And Women Of God Arise In The Workplace And Conquer! How To Navigate The Seas Of Envy, Jealousy And Sabotage."* As I wrote that book, here are some lessons I learned as it relates to the writing process:

- Writing a book does not happen overnight. The process of completing a book can take months, even years. It is, thus, important for you to stick to the process, stay committed and focused.

- Sometimes the desire to write or finish your book is innate. It is your passion to write content that inspires, empowers, and encourages. It is your passion to write, period. When you are passionate about writing, the rest becomes easier because you possess the desire to simply write. There is a pleasure that is intrinsic when you start to type or write in a book or on paper about the ideas that are circulating in your mind. However, the point is, get the ideas out of your mind. Make them visible to be read by others.

- Ideas about your writing project can strike anytime, so be prepared. While on the go, use your cellphone to jot down ideas that may strike. Have a notebook and pen as well to write down what pops up in your head randomly. Your laptop and tablet are devices that can also be used for storing your ideas. If you do not have time to develop your ideas, just jot them down. Expand on them when you do have the time.

- Set up a schedule to work on your book. Choose days you have designated as time allotted or slotted to work towards completing your book.

- Be persistent, if not consistent, in working on your writing projects.

I believe in the power of prayer. I wanted to write a book but had no idea what to write about, so I asked God to give me an idea. He also gave me the idea for this book.

- What do I write about?

Your experiences. Your expertise. Your knowledge about a specific topic, service, product, or business. Your passion. You. Write what YOU feel will touch others. Write about what you love. Write about what you abhor. JUST WRITE!

- Who will be interested in buying it?

Someone wants to read what you have written. There are things that have occurred in your life that have happened to others, and they want to know how you overcame it or how you are dealing with it. Adversity and opposition is not an individual occurrence; it is global. We are scattered across the seven continents but connected through the imperfections of life.

- A book is like a professionally written essay. It takes multiple drafts to reach your idea of perfection. So, be prepared to write. Then rewrite. Then change. Then add. Then delete. Then rearrange. Then do the process repeatedly until completed.

- Depending on the topic, do some research, so the information presented has more credibility.

The Publishing Process

When I completed my first book, I contemplated publishing it independently. I chose not to do this because I realized how much time went into the process after I did the research. I did not have the time. I was a teacher and a tutor who tutored on weekends and weekdays. I, thus, opted to pay for the process.

What I learnt about this process:

- Choose a publishing company that represents what you have written about.

Do your research. Look at the reviews. Compare prices but ensure that the services offered by whomever you choose personify excellence and professionalism.

- Send in your manuscript and wait to see if they will accept it.

- There is a back-and-forth process where you will have to reread what your editor has edited to make sure that what they have corrected is still grammatically accurate. You want to put a book out that reads well, and the message may be hindered in being conveyed if it reads poorly.

- After you have written your book, it may take another six months to be published. It depends on how quickly the company works and how quickly you pay.

Everybody's publishing experience will be different. I just related what my first experience was.

Marketing Your Book

Let me state succinctly that I was never one who was active on social media. Call me silly, but I perceived social media as an avenue for others to pry and see what was happening in your life. I value my privacy, and having never indulged or engaged in social media, I never perceived it as a tool that could be used to showcase or share with the public about my book.

So, here are a few tools that you may use to market your book:

- Instagram
- Facebook

- Tik Tok
- YouTube
- Radio stations
- Television networks
- Newspaper agencies
- Book stores
- Book launch
- Word of mouth
- Reviews (encourage whomever purchases to leave a review on any platform they purchased)
- Flyers

6
Educate Yourself

If you are in the business of teaching, then you should definitely be in the business of learning. There is a teacher in all of us. We share knowledge and information with others in some capacity and show others how to get things done, whether you are a parent, manager, employer, pastor, colleague, sibling, or child. You teach from the perspective of what you know; thus, it is imperative to keep expanding your current repertoire of intellect. Granted, some are better teachers than others because of perhaps training or just possessing a natural knack.

While waiting to be wed, why not go back to school? Why not do a course online or in a school setting? Why not do that diploma, degree, or doctorate? Why not be one level up educationally?

Is money a factor? Then why not sign up for workshops? Why not do free courses and accumulate certificates in content that interests you and can be beneficial?

Is time a factor? There are twenty-four hours in a day. You do need to rest. However, if in your free time you are complaining about having not yet found your spouse or daydreaming about who your future spouse will be, then you have time to do a course. When your mind is gainfully occupied with bettering yourself, then less time is spent assessing your singlehood.

If you choose to go back to school, here are some things to consider:

- What will be your area of focus academically? Why?

- Is what you want to pursue marketable or a waste of money? Do not waste money, even if you are in a financial position to. It is a precious commodity. Do not waste your time. Do not just start a course to "pass the time." Be actively engaged and invested. Choose something that will be an asset.

- If you must take a loan, how is your current financial situation? You may want to go back to school, but if you already have a student loan that you need to pay off, you may have to wait, not cancel, just postpone momentarily. You do not want to be in further debt. You may have a high mortgage or be a single parent, so you do not have extra cash at your disposal for now. Whatever the case may be, assess your financial situation before enrolling in an educational institution.

- What works better for you? Is it online or being in a physical classroom?

If you choose online, remember self-discipline is necessary. You will have to remember when to log on for various classes and when assignments are due. If you are a busy individual, you will need to schedule these tasks on a calendar for reminders.

- If you choose to be in a physical space (a classroom), be practical and sensible. Assess the proximity of your chosen location for classes to home. Will you experience burnout if you have to commute or drive to and from classes after work? Are your traveling expenses affordable or outside your budget?

- If you choose to go back to school, get your certification from a reputable institution. Make sure the course you choose to complete is accredited. The last thing you need is to start and finish a programme that you may never get paid for.

- You will not just need time to complete assignments, but you will need time to complete them well. Whatever you choose to do, excel in it. Finish with excellence, not mediocrity.

7
Find Another Stream Of Income

Whether this was something you thought about or not, COVID-19 has made everyone struggle financially and begin to contemplate multiple streams of income. Bills are piling up, and hours at work for many have decreased. In the same breath, many have become unemployed.

However, what if you could save more money to put towards your wedding? Some women already have their exquisite wedding gowns ready to be purchased. The venue is already mentally booked, and the imaginary bridesmaids and guests have already been invited. They just have not received the invitation yet.

I have learnt not to limit what I can do to make money. You may discover hidden talents because of your persistence and consistency. Here are some things you may consider doing:

- Online selling: Sell your own products.

- Tutoring services: Online, home

- Author

- Teaching position: Teacher/Coaching

- YouTube Creator: Connect to Google AdSense. When people click on ads, you will earn money from AdSense. Gain popularity and companies will pay you to review their product. You may even become the "face" for a specific brand: hair, fashion, make-up, singlehood, single parenting, travel vlogs, family vlogs, driving lessons, spiritual content, comical. Choose something you enjoy doing and go for it! Just ensure that it glorifies God. Let everything be done in decency and in order.

- Exercise Instructor

- Dog Walker

- Pet Sitting

- Do you like to bake? Sell your goodies.

- Sell t-shirts

- Event Planner

- Seamstress

- Airbnb: You can rent out your home or a room to vacationers. It goes without saying, however, that during COVID-19, this is illegal and unwise. This pandemic, hopefully, will dissipate one day and make this a viable option once more.

- Uber services

- Bookkeeping

- Start a cleaning company

- Launch your clothing line

- Editor

- Affiliate marketing: Use your active website or blog to promote certain products/services on your site and receive a flat rate or percentage of the amount of what was sold.

- Write an e-book.

- Invest in things that give you royalties, such as books, music, or screenwriting.

- Invest in stocks.

- Photography: You may love taking pictures, so your passion can bring extra income. Advertise through social media and other avenues.

- Become a silent business partner: If you do not have the time to start your own business, invest in a small, successful business and partake in the profits.

- Open your own practice: If you cannot afford an office space, work from home. If you own your house, transform your basement or an empty room into an office.

- If you have a beautiful voice, book yourself to sing at events.

- Try to land a gig doing voiceovers. There are tons of voice-over tips on YouTube.

If there is anything you are considering but not sure how to proceed, YOUTUBE is an excellent resource that caters to the different learning styles, such as Kinesthetic, Visual, Auditory, Verbal, Social, Solitary, and Logical.

Additionally, you can consider another method, which is outlined in the next chapter.

Here are some advantages of having another stream of income:

- If you lose your 9-5, you have another means of income until you get back on your feet.

- Your other means of income may become the avenue through which you launch into ownership/entrepreneurship.

- It reduces financial stress as the risk lessens to being left without an income.

- You can save more.

- The extra cash can be used to pay off loans, outstanding debt, mortgage faster.

- You have a holiday fund. When it is time to vacation, you do not have to rely on your credit card.

- You can stick to your morals and values. You do not have to date or sleep with anyone for cash; thus, exercising abstinence.

- You have more money when you retire at your disposal.

- You will build wealth long-term as you earn more than you spend and your passive income (money you make while you are sleeping) gradually increases.

- If your extra income excites you, it can decrease boredom at work. It is something to look forward to.

- Your extra stream of income may be something you want to do full-time and so motivates you to work harder at it so you can quit your 9-5.

You can generate extra income based on your passion, interests, and talents. However, finding another stream of income can be time-consuming, tedious, and expensive. Do not let this deter you. CONSISTENCY equals PROFICIENCY, which leads to INTENSITY in making your idea or dreams a reality.

If ideas are currently circulating as to how you can make money, quickly grab a pen or pencil and jot them down. Do not lose that train of thought.

8
Read Books

Why are you currently reading this book? For knowledge? Out of boredom? Curiosity? Excitement?

People read for different reasons, but perhaps you are reading this book because you are single, and the title piqued your interest. You may be reading because you have read something I have written before, and you like my writing style. You may have bought this book because you want to support me and ended up reading it. Whatever the reason, thank you for reading, and thank you for leaving a review (hint).

As mentioned in the previous chapter, one thing you can do as you wait to get married is try to earn another income, and one way to get more knowledge about this is investing in books that specifically give you strategies and tools that you can use to get multiple streams of income. Books can be the "how-to" guide on or about any topic that interests you.

Here are some advantages of reading:

- Improves and increases your word choice or vocabulary. It makes you more intelligent.

- When you read, your mind is actively engaged, which strengthens the brain and may lower the risk of dementia and Alzheimer.

- Travel vicariously through books. Love to travel but cannot? Read a book about where you would like to visit. Do not want to buy books? Then go to the library. It is a little outdated, I know, but still relevant. You may also download the free kindle app and download a travel book you may like for free if you are impatient to wait on a paperback. You can get it electronically in seconds.

- You will sleep better. If you are tired but cannot sleep, pick up a book.

- Reduces stress. Reading is relaxing.

- Increases your comprehension skills.

- Makes you a better writer and conversationalist as it stimulates your imagination and stirs up new ideas, hence, your creativity.

- Reading improves focus and concentration.

- It also improves your memory.

- Your children or siblings may exemplify you. Be a role model for something positive.

- It can build your self-confidence.

- Empowers you to understand and be more accepting of others.

- It is enjoyable.

If you do not know which book to start reading, then I suggest The Holy Bible. There is no question that you have that the Bible cannot answer. You only need to believe and search.

After that, go do some searching on the internet as to which is the best book to read to meet your present needs.

Reading, for me personally, has provided escapism. I caution, though, be mindful of the content that you feed your mind through words. Words have power. Feed your mind with words that will make you a better person and thinker. Avoid books that will feed the flesh, give you an insatiable appetite for sex, worldly possessions, and thoughts. I am very selective of the content that I read and watch because the subconscious actively internalizes what is seen, and it comes to the surface in subtle and sometimes destructive ways.

Read with understanding. The ability to read is powerful, but the capacity to understand and apply what you have read is a gift from God. Reading opens your mind to possibilities. A wise person reads.

9
Travel

Immersing in another culture is beautiful. I love to travel. When you step through the doors of an airport, there is an exhilarating feeling that is unmatched. You are filled with awe and curiosity as you delve into newness and the unknown. There are so many other countries that I want to visit and, by God's grace, I will.

Traveling is not just to keep your mind off your singlehood, but rather you can experience the following:

- Improved health.

Travelling is not only relaxing but therapeutic. You can write from experience; first world countries can be filled with smog, pollution, too many people, and food that is not really organic, but you pay exorbitant prices for. When I return to the island of my birth, the crisp, fresh mountain air is refreshing and clean. When you inhale, you feel the oxygen in your lungs. When you step in the market, you pick up produce that still have the land's dirt on it. The soil is so rich and is either vibrantly red or dark in colour. My skin, hair, and nails begin to thrive even more, and I get the flu less, and the hustle and bustle of a fast-paced economy fade as I acclimatize to a less rigid and freer flow. Travelling is medicinal. Backaches, sore feet, muscles, and tendons disappear, and your joints feel more supple, and you move with more fluidity and grace. It is a spa treatment that every human being deserves.

Nature is also at its best. When I look at trees, feel or sit in the grass, I feel a sense of peace and tranquility that evokes joy and contentment. Happiness is free, and the more of it you experience, the better your health will be, so travel.

- Traveling makes you smarter: You gain knowledge about the customs, values, and belief system of a society, essentially their culture.

- Traveling makes your conversations more interesting: You will have something to talk about with your future spouse. Your love for traveling might be something you share in common. Who knows?

- If you are a food lover, traveling will definitely give you a taste of different cuisines and broaden the horizons of your palette.

- You become Dora or Diego, the Explorer. How adventurous are you as you travel the globe? You will not only look like an adventurer but feel like one too, and guess what? Your traveling may lead to you creating vlogs for YouTube or blogging; hence, increasing your following so when you are ready to sell a product/service, viola! You can advertise to your huge group of followers. Travelling will also provide you with something to maybe write and publish about.

- You learn a new language.

- You learn skills like adjusting, socializing, and accepting differences about diversity. When you travel, you become less judgmental, stereotypical, biased, and prejudiced.

- You make new friends.

- Perhaps start a new career as a travel consultant.

- A respite from a stressful job.

- FUN!

You do not have to leave your country to travel; you can travel on a budget and without a passport or visa. There are hidden gems in your country to discover and old places to revisit.

How to explore your own country:

- Perceive things through the eyes of a tourist. Where do they like to visit? Go there.

- Do you know the history of your country? Visit the museum, libraries, old war sites, caves, archaeological sites, etc.

- Have an open mind.

- Be genuinely curious.

- Have a spirit of adventure.

- Good company makes everything better.

- Get a tour guide.

- Go on a tour bus.

- Look for moments to LIVE and LAUGH.

Advantages of exploring your own country:

- You spend within your country, and so boost the economy.

- You learn more about your country as you interact with your people, the locals.

- You spend less: no airfare or perhaps hotel and car rental fees.

- You become more patriotic and appreciative of your culture.

- You can travel with your family or friends and improve bonds and friendships. Not to say you cannot travel together outside of the country, but it may not have been possible for numerous reasons, such as a lack of funds, travel restrictions, health factors, aerophobia (fear of flying), just to name a few.

- It may stimulate ideas for writing a book or books.

- You may meet people who become lifelong friends and/or business partners.

- You are creating great memories in the land of your birth and harnessing stories to share with your children and grandchildren.

- You may just meet your future spouse.

10
Volunteer

Not everything you do has to be done with an expectation or desire for monetary gain. Acts 20:35 states, *"...it is more blessed to give than to receive." (ESV)*. There are so many non-profit, private, and charitable organizations in need of help but lack the funds to hire the necessary support staff. You could be the answer to someone's prayer.

In addition, there are various shelters—the homeless, single, abused, orphanages, and teenage pregnancy homes that you can offer your time and make a difference in someone's life. There are also nursing homes, after-school programs, Sunday school, youth gatherings, etc.

Here are some benefits of volunteering:

- It improves your mood.

- It makes you happy and, therefore, combats stress.

- It fosters the growth of empathy and sympathy, which makes us more human.

- It fosters feelings of gratitude and thankfulness.

- It provides an avenue through which you can give love and kindness while, in turn, receiving both.

- You make new and "old" friends. Pun intended.

- It looks good on your resume.

- You are gaining experience for free, which can assist or come in handy for future jobs.

- It can be a workout and so good for you physically, especially if you have a desk job.

- You may meet your future spouse at the very place you are volunteering. God works in mysterious way. As you freely give to others, He blesses you in turn.

- It motivates you to get out of bed and be less selfish and a complainer.

- It teaches you how to love, not just with words and speech, but with action and truth.

- It teaches you how to serve and, therefore, be more humble. In order to be a great leader, you must first learn how to serve others.

- You are obeying God's Word, which states you are to help the weak, poor, and needy (See Psalm 41:1).

- You learn how to do good for others without expecting something in return from people who are not in a position to give back. What a breath of fresh air you will be when the majority appears self-seeking and selfish.

- When you spend your time in the company of those who are oppressed, you can lead them to Jesus. As you let your light shine, God will be glorified.

- As you give freely, you gain intrinsically.

How do we find volunteer opportunities?

- Through your church.

- Through your present employer.

- If you currently volunteer and want to do more, ask the organization that you are currently at to point you to more places.

- Through your school (if attending).

- Think about your values; identify the urgent needs in society currently, and put your skillset to helpful use.

If you choose to volunteer, do not burn yourself out. You are only human. Take on only what you can manage.

Jesus gave His services freely. He performed countless miracles and never charged a dollar. By volunteering, He impacted so many lives and changed the course of history permanently. No one has given their life and made it possible for sinners when they repented to be in heaven, and no one can. He sacrificed His life, and His reward is now that He is sitting at the right hand of God. What a promotion!

My point is this, if you are a believer, who loves God, and obey His Word, then if you volunteer here on earth, rest assured your Father sees and will reward you in this life and the next. For when you help others, you show them that Jesus is alive.

Volunteer with LOVE and watch how your perspective on life changes, brightens, and become more optimistic.

11
Find A Cause That You Are Passionate About And Get Invested

Finding a cause gives you purpose.
Purpose gives you hope.
Hope gives you joy.
Joy gives you a reason to wake up each morning.

There are so many advertisements that show children suffering on continents that are perhaps so far away from you, when in your own backyard, there are men, women, and children who are in dire and desperate need of your monetary support. If you have cash to spare, then you do not have to hoard it or be a spendthrift that buys frivolous things you really have no use for. Donate it to a worthy cause.

If you are struggling to figure out which organization to give to, perhaps these questions can aid you:

- What is your current occupation? Give within your field of expertise or experience.

- Do you love what you do? If you love what you do for a living, you may wish to give cash within that area.

- Do you have a desire to help the poor, sick, abused, neglected, orphaned, or elderly? If none of those kinds of people, then who?

- Do you attend church?

- Is there an area in your church that you see requires financial assistance?

- How about a school in your community or a daycare center? Do they need financial support?

- Is there a homeless person you want to help get back on their feet?

- Is there someone you want to help because they are behind on their mortgage or rent and may face eviction?

- Is there a child who is smart and requires financial assistance to go to school?

- Are you in a position to give supplies like food, pencils, backpacks, and clothing to an organization monthly?

- Are you able to buy groceries for a poor family monthly until they get back on their feet?

- Can you take care of a phone bill for someone who is struggling financially?

Have you ever been in need? I have, and I wished desperately for money to cover bills that were accumulating. I lost my job, and because of COVID-19, for the first time in my life, I was unemployed for ten months. I was alone in a foreign country, and the job sector was not hiring. Every cent I had saved was dwindling, and I had no one to help me.

My point is this: if you see someone in need, help him or her.

There are also charities you can give to. Here is a list; you choose:

- The Breast Cancer Research Foundation (or any cancer society you choose).

- American Humane (or any animal organization you choose; just presenting an idea).

- The Alzheimer's Association (or any irreversible, progressive brain disorder you choose).

- Sick Kids Foundation.

- Habitat for Humanity.

- Bustamante Hospital for Children.

Please note, I am not saying donate to these organizations. I am merely planting an idea as to where you can give your money. Please do thorough research before you give to any organization, even in your hometown. You do not want to give to dishonest people.

What if you cannot donate monthly but can afford to give a one-time monetary contribution? That is commendable and better than nothing. Give what you can, if you can. If money is what you want to give but cannot at the moment, ask God to bless you financially so you will be able to give. However, in the meantime, volunteer.

What are the possible benefits of donating? You will experience similar benefits to volunteering, but here are a few that you may not have thought of:

- You can help your own community to make their way out of poverty.

- This should not be the reason you give, but you can get it back on your tax returns. What you give is tax refundable, depending on the country you live in.

- If you are a business owner, it is free publicity.

- If you are a business owner, you gain customer support and respect even more.

- If you donate as a company, it increases employees' work ethics and morale. It increases work spirit, positivity, and pride in being employed at such a generous company.

When donating, you can call or check out the organization's website. Read about their mission statement; which part of the world do they assist or have existing branches? You can then decipher how you want to give if it is by cheque or online or simply ask them how you can give. If possible, visit their headquarters and see if they are reputable and legit. It is your money; you have the right to investigate.

These are not just the benefits of donating; you may give and discover a plethora of so much more.

If there is nothing here that interests you, then you can start your own GoFundMe or nonprofit organization. There may be a cause that you believe is not discussed enough. For example, you may also be passionate about how people die each year, and you want to use your organization to spread awareness. It may also be about an ailment, illness or disease that is within your family, so your cause is a personal one. Find YOUR cause and get invested!

12
Learn A New Skill

A skill is something you learn, and over a period of time, you gain the ability, competence, and experience to do it well and perhaps master it.

Marriage is even more beautiful when you find the one who compliments your purpose. When you marry, your purpose does too, for better or worse. When you first marry, it is like learning a new skill. You must learn to share your space with someone, adjust to their temperament and figure out how to coexist as one. Marriage is a skill that, when mastered, brings rewards that never end.

Here are some skills you will need for your marriage to be successful:

- Communication
- Compromise
- Trust
- Forgiveness
- Time Management
- Thankfulness
- Respect
- Conflict Resolution

- Affection, hospitality, and kindness
- Servitude (If you hate serving others, then marriage is not for you as you will be serving your husband/wife for life. It does not make you a servant. You both will be serving each other, and that makes you his/her partner. Please note, wives, God created you to be a helpmeet to your husband, not his doormat. Do not tolerate being mistreated or abused in any way, whether psychological, emotional, physical, mental, or social. Men, this is also applicable to you).
- Truthfulness
- Fidelity (If you cannot be faithful, do not get involved or marry anyone. However, after marriage, you have pledged to be with one person till death before witnesses and God, so if you know you are not ready to commit FULLY, then do not do it).
- Be an unselfish lover to your spouse.
- Fear of God.

While waiting for marriage, the above are things you can develop if you think you are lacking or need to improve. No matter how well you think you know your partner, you will truly get to know them when you live together.

Here are some skills you can work on before marriage:

- Dependability
- Reliability
- Punctuality
- Budgeting; saving not squandering.
- Humility
- Agreeability (not a quarrelsome individual)
- Active listener

- Patience
- Stress management (How do you handle pressure? Are you a quitter? Do you disappear for days? Do you get angry or non-responsive?).
- Decision-making (Are you indecisive? Always wavering? Make decisions and stick to them? A person can always change their mind, but if they do it too often, then today they will choose to love you, and tomorrow they decide not to).

- Loving and lovable (women, be feminine, be kind, be compassionate, be human, and men, reciprocate with respect and appreciation).

Which of the above skills do you think you need to work on? Whatever you choose, begin to work on it while you are single, not when you are married. Dating can bring out the best in you, but marriage can bring out the worst in you. Do not let that be the case as it relates to your marriage!

You can always learn something new because there is always room for individual improvement. Whatever skill you choose to learn, it may or can become so much more than a pastime but could also be another means of income, for example:

- Embroidery
- Crocheting or knitting
- Sewing
- Playing chess
- Self-defense courses, just to name a few

There is also Skilled Industrial Trades such as welders, machinists, and mechanics.

Skilled Construction Trades: electricians, plumbers, carpenters, technicians.

Skilled Service Trades: Nurses, aides, orderlies, therapists, service technicians.

These skilled jobs pay well, and if you are thinking of migrating from a third-world country to a first-world country, then being a skilled worker can work advantageously for you. One of the above professions will make you even more marketable, especially in the skilled industrial and construction trades. There is a demand for such individuals.

Here are some benefits of learning a new skill:

- Creativity
- Ingenuity
- Independence/Solitary play/Self-esteem
- Self-actualization
- Adaptability/Learn another skill more quickly.
- Patience
- You learn or develop qualities like consistency, persistence, and determination.
- Improve your knowledge.
- A sense of accomplishment and pride.
- Access to new opportunities/networking.
- Stress reliever

You may choose to brush up on your driving skills and, thus, learn how to drive a bus, truck, or forklift. Being a bus driver or truck driver can provide extra income, and learning how to operate a forklift can give you money from another source as well. In some first-world countries, the pay is fantastic, and there is a wonderful pension package for bus drivers.

13
Change Your Career

Over the years, I have experienced burnout, not so much as a teacher, but as an Early Childhood Educator. The bending and lifting placed much pressure on my lower back. Both professions can take a toll on your body physically and emotionally, and I contemplated many times changing my career, but because I love imparting knowledge, I have not changed my profession. However, I pose the question to you, do you really love what you do? Do you feel an intrinsic reward? Do you wake up each morning wanting to go to work, or are you dragging your feet? Do you see yourself everyday working somewhere else? Have you contemplated a new career?

A career change, to me, is such a greater transition than just merely changing your job. If you change your job, it can be within the same field, but you are broadening your horizons exponentially through a whole new knowledge and skill set when you change your career. For example, from a teacher to an electrician, or a bus driver to a professor, that is a new career; the two are not closely related. Nevertheless, when you are a manager in Toronto and then take up another managerial position in Vancouver, you simply relocated, but your job remains the same.

A career change is, therefore, greater than a job change. It is like getting a profession make-over. You went to bed as a janitor and woke up a lawyer. That is so not impossible! So, are you ready for a career change?

Is there something you have always wanted to do but never got around to doing it? Do not procrastinate anymore.

Some of the reasons I have changed my job over the years are:

- No room for promotion.
- No benefits (dental, health).
- There was no challenge. There was a monotony to the daily tasks, and absolute boredom began to set in.
- Being a supervisor and overseeing a staff older than you is absolute stress. I try to avoid stress. It is not good for your health, skin, hair, nails. Stress kills!
- The pay was insufficient.
- My talents were underused or were used or exploited without a raise in pay.
- My bosses wanted too much for too little.
- Simple words like "Thank you" and "I appreciate you" were uttered but not shown by colleagues or employers. Staff Appreciation Day, for example, goes a very long way in my eyes. It is not always about the money.

If you want to make a career change, then go for it!

Do you want to make a career change but not sure what to choose? Let us do an assessment:

1. If you want to change your career, write your top five choices.

    1. _____
    2. _____
    3. _____
    4. _____
    5. _____

2. Do some research. Based on your research, what are the top five jobs that are in demand in the country you wish to work, and will not decline in need over the next ten years? This means the market for such jobs is secure because employers will always be hiring. You thus have options as it relates to where you want to work because the job market is not saturated.

    - _____
    - _____
    - _____
    - _____
    - _____

3. Write your five main reasons for wanting a career change.

    1. _____
    2. _____
    3. _____
    4. _____
    5. _____

If you are desirous of a career change, think about the following:

- Are you willing to return to school?
- Are you willing to relocate, if necessary, to where greater opportunities are based on your career choice?
- What is the duration or length of the course? What is the projected graduation date? Can you make it shorter?

Things that should NOT deter you from starting a new career:

- Age: It is never too late until you are dead.
- Child/ren
- Divorce
- An ex
- Parents
- Friends
- Your current fiancé
- Fear of failure
- Setbacks

The only limitations that exist are in your mind. Remember that—advocate for your future.

14
Get Healthier

Do you even need a reason to improve your health? If you wish to marry, make sure you are working on living a certain lifestyle that will place you in the best possible shape for your future spouse. No one knows when they are going to die. Death is beyond our control; we may be so healthy and then fly on a plane that plunges into the Atlantic Ocean. While you are in the land of the living, take care of you!

I read a book years ago titled "Eating Right for Your Type" by Dr. Peter J.D'Adamo, and it has changed my life ever since. Of course, if you are thinking of purchasing this book, then I suggest finding out your blood type first if you do not already know. This book basically categorizes food into three groups: neutral, medicinal, and poisonous. These groupings are based on your blood type, so it informs you about the kind of food that will be great, terrible, or has no effect on the body at all. For individuals struggling with maintaining the right weight, this book can aid you in doing just that as it will point you in the direction as to which foods to avoid. Most importantly, as you eat right for your blood type, you will experience a healthier body, mind, and spirit as food is the sustenance of life, not just physically but mentally.

Everything must be consumed in moderation. Eat to live, not live to eat. Eating healthy does not mean tasteless and unappetizing food. However, it may mean that you must retrain your taste buds and palette to consume less sugar and salt or find healthier alternatives.

When your body feels good, you feel good about yourself. Your mindset is healthier, and you are more prepared to have and maintain healthy relationships. Before you meet your spouse, ensure you are surrounded by people who give you a peace of mind and spirit. Healthy, platonic friendships will provide a loving, supportive, and nurturing environment for you to pursue you as you wait patiently for God's best.

Getting healthier means:

- Improving your diet.
- Exercising.
- Giving up unhealthy habits, like smoking and drinking.
- Practicing good posture.
- Distancing/avoiding the formulation or maintenance of poisonous friendships.
- Speaking positively. Words have power. Speak life, blessings, and positive affirmations. Speaking positively will lead to having a positive outlook on life.
- Spending more quiet time with God (most essential).
- Getting sufficient sleep.

A healthier body is equivalent to a healthier mind, and, thus, you are more prepared to handle a relationship that will lead to marriage. Being beautiful is great, but if your mind is not, I am not sorry, but you are most ugly and extremely unattractive. Make sure your beauty is not just superficial but transcends beyond what is visible. A good heart is stunning!

One of the things that you may begin focusing on if you do not know where to start is looking at what you are genetically predisposed to. What diseases/issues run in your family? Is it high blood pressure? High cholesterol? Fibromyalgia? Infertility issues? Obesity? Anorexia nervosa? Do not try to address these issues when you start having health problems. Address them before you must visit the doctor. Start to make the necessary changes to your diet to curb or stop later health issues.

Does alcoholism run in your family? If it does, then pace yourself when you drink or abstain. If it is high blood pressure, then fried foods must be eliminated or avoided. Is it being overweight? Watch what you consume. Find healthy alternatives to satisfy your cravings or appetite. Do what is within your control as you ask God to strengthen you and give you greater self-control.

As much as is possible, give yourself a fighting chance to not only expand your life but to live a long and healthy one. You want the energy to do things with and for your spouse. You need the vitality for your child/ren. Life happens, but you want the moments you spend with your spouse to be living life outside of doctor's visits, hospitals, and medical fees. Again, I write, you and I have no control over whether we will get sick or not; however, still try to prolong your life by trying to seek, establish and maintain a healthy state and mind as much as is humanly possible.

As it relates to exercise, as mentioned before, you do not have to join a gym to exercise. There are tons of workout videos on

YouTube, Play Store apps, and Google. Type in your requests, and what pops up will leave you with many choices. After a while, your search engine will automatically generate videos like what you have typed in as it has stored your interests, so you will have an even more expansive selection list.

15
Mend Broken Family Relationships

Your family is a precious gift from God. You were placed within a family unit so you would not have to share successes and failures alone. Love is present in every family, even if it is from only one member.

A family does not have to be biological; it can be a church family, a work family, or even a group of friends that treat you better than blood. It has been my experience that my love from my family has grown as I have aged. When I was younger, I did not see the beauty of their affection, nor did I feel it. It took traveling and being away from home for years and finally returning broke, jobless and ill to see what I thought was missing when I left: LOVE. My story is like "The Prodigal Son," but instead, as I am a female, the story is titled "The Prodigal Daughter."

Before you marry, fix situations within your family unit before you bring your spouse home to introduce to anyone. Your spouse will want to meet your family. He/she will want to travel back to see your roots, where you grew up, and who you really are, and get to know you on a deeper level. You can learn quite a lot about an individual through their family unit simply by observing how they interact with their siblings, cousins, parents, grandparents. Ladies and gentlemen, if your future spouse is disrespectful to his/her parents, then that is an indicator that he/she will be disrespectful to you too. What your future spouse may never have shared about their past: a particular idea, attribute, or characteristic may become evident when you see them conversing in a family setting.

Mending broken family relationships will make you raise your child/ren in a more supportive family circle. Give your child/ren stability; they deserve it.

Here are some benefits of fixing broken family relationships:

- Inner Peace
- Relief
- Joy
- A closer bond arises/develops with said family member/s.
- If the person dies unexpectedly, you will not feel regret because you made peace with him/her before he/she passed.
- Peaceful and joyous family gatherings.
- A deeper sense of belonging.
- A strengthening in communicating and, hence, not keeping family secrets.
- More laughter, which is medicinal.
- Emotional and social support.
- Assistance if necessary during financially hard times.
- Attendees at your wedding that you know (lol).
- More wedding gifts. (Yes, it is better to give than receive, but it does not hurt to get).

How to approach mending broken relationships:

- Pray about the situation.
- Be the bigger person; start the conversation first.
- Discuss as calmly as possible what caused the rift and what offended you.
- Give it time but be persistent.
- Forgive: it may be difficult but do not just try, do it.
- If necessary, seek counseling as a family; no shame in that.
- Send a gift. It can be as simple as a card that tells how you feel. Be sincere and state what you are apologizing about. You may choose to send a bouquet.

Sometimes a family relationship is broken because of a deep, dark secret like rape, molestation, etc. Forgive who did it to you and forgive who never believed you when you told. Talking to the individual/s who did such a despicable action may prove to be the most difficult thing to do. I encourage you to start off with prayer, but let go of the hurt and pain, and give yourself permission to heal, even if you are reluctant, refuse to, or cannot talk to those who hurt you.

If your efforts of reconciliation are met consistently with rejection, do not give up, but know when you may jeopardize your health and pull back. It is more than okay to forgive and love from a distance.

If you extend peace and gratitude to a family member and they do not accept it, then remember the Word of God states: *"If it be possible, as much as in you lieth, be at peace with ALL men." (Romans 12:18 - ASV)*. Please focus on "as much as lieth in you." That means there are limitations on how much you can get from another person when you offer peace. You cannot force someone to accept your peace offering and, in turn, render their forgiveness.

However, you will experience an inner peace and a free conscience to move forward without their forgiveness with gratitude and love.

Another scripture in Exodus 14:14 also states: *"The LORD shall fight for you, and ye shall hold your peace." (KJV)*. The Amplified Bible states: *"The LORD will fight for you while you [only need to] keep silent and remain calm."*

Some battles are won by your composed nature and your silence because God will do the fighting and you know He has never lost a battle.

16
Learn A New Sport

Learning is an exhilarating feeling, and if you are truly invested, it can be a very pleasurable and unforgettable experience. The great thing with technology is that you can go online and teach yourself without leaving the confines of your home and without paying a dime, a cent, or a nickel.

Have you ever wanted to ski? Do rock climbing? Become a pro at playing chess? Football? Cricket? Basketball? Volleyball? Baseball? Synchronized swimming? The opportunity to do just that is very much possible right now.

One of the things as human beings that we should strive to do is pick up good habits. We want to get into the habit of doing things that benefit our minds, bodies, and spirit. Formulating good habits require consistent training. Train yourself to do constructive actions that will build a better you tomorrow internally and so transcend externally and, thus, make you an appealing company.

Outlined below are some physical benefits of learning a new sport:

- Improve your stamina.
- Get you fit.

- Improve your gross and fine motor skills.
- Possibly stave off ailments that affect the brain, like dementia and Alzheimer.
- Get your heart stronger.
- Make you sweat, which is a great thing.
- Help you to lose weight.
- Tone your muscles.
- Take you out of your comfort zone and challenge you physically and mentally.
- Good reflexes, improving your reaction time.
- Improves your focus.
- A great way to channel pent up energy, hostility and aggression.
- Develop skills like respect, resilience, and discipline.

Learning a new sport can also benefit you socially. Here are a few advantages:

- Make new friends.
- Improve your communication skills.
- Teach you how to start up conversations with strangers.
- Cooperative skills/working together to win.
- How to accept losses.
- Anger management.
- Unity.
- Exposes you to different personality types. You learn to work with them, which is a beneficial skill to possess in order to co-exist in this world.

17
Develop A Relationship With Yourself

Who I am today and how I perceive myself currently was not always how I saw myself. When I looked in the mirror as a teenager, I saw the things I did not like and never the things I loved about myself. I saw what I was not good at and never what I could excel at.

When my self-esteem bloomed and blossomed, and I received a compliment, I no longer wondered if someone meant it when it was spoken because my self-worth no longer required validation, because I was now in love with myself.

When an individual has no clue who they are, they may seek their value in self-destructive actions, such as:

- Multiple sex partners
- Meaningless sex
- Substance abuse
- Lies to get attention
- Risky adrenalin-filled activities
- Self-sabotaging relationships
- Frequent fights and brawls
- Binging

- Overeating
- Starving oneself
- Anti-social/isolation
- Drinking too much

The above behaviours are self-destructive as they destroy the essence, identity, and spirit of who you truly are. You become a shell of who God really created you to be. Your potential is minimized because your mind is filled with limitations.

Let us do a quiz. Grab a pen/pencil.

1. Who are you?

_____
_____
_____
_____

2. What do you like?

_____
_____
_____
_____

3. Do you change to suit the person you are dating? Who is your best friend at the time?

_____
_____
_____
_____

4. What are your pet peeves?

_____
_____
_____
_____

5. What are your idiosyncrasies?

_____
_____
_____
_____

6. What are your strengths in a relationship?

_____
_____
_____
_____

7. What will you not accept or tolerate in a relationship?

_____
_____
_____
_____

8. What are your likes and dislikes?

_____
_____
_____

9. Are you afraid to vocalize your needs?
_____
_____
_____
_____

10. Will you always push your feelings aside or sweep it under a rug to please others and so suffer in misery quietly?
_____
_____
_____
_____

11. Are you a self-motivated individual?
_____
_____

12. Do you need to be pushed or cajoled?
_____
_____

13. Are you determined?
_____
_____

14. Do you give up easily?
_____
_____

15. Are you territorial or possessive when in a relationship? Has it been an issue in the past?
_____
_____

16. Do you get jealous easily? Men, are you attracted to the femme fatale type? Ladies, are you attracted to the bad boy persona?
_____
_____

17. Have you always settled? Do you think you deserve the best?
_____
_____

18. Do you like staying home or going out?
_____
_____

19. Do you often say yes when you mean no?
_____
_____

20. Do you allow people to take advantage of your kindness?
_____
_____

21. What are your most positive qualities?
_____
_____
_____
_____

22. What are your not-so-attractive qualities?
_____
_____
_____
_____

23. Have you cheated on your partner while in a relationship?
_____
_____

24. Have you been cheated on?
_____
_____

Depending on what your responses are to the above questions, you may have some work to do on yourself before you find your spouse or your spouse finds you.

Biblical affirmations are a great way to build or rebuild your self-worth. My YouTube Channel @Kadeen Dobbs has such videos that you can listen to daily.

When you know yourself, then you know what to look for in a lifetime partner. When you know yourself, you will not get lost pretending to be someone you are not.

18
Save: Get Your Finances In Order

As you age, the mortality of life looms boldly in your thoughts as a reminder that life must be approached with more circumspect and wisdom. When you were younger, you did not think about death too much. When you were extremely young, you did not even understand the concept. You tried daring acts because there was such fearlessness. As you age and people started to address you by saying, "Yes, ma'am" or "Excuse me, sir," you may begin to ponder how and when did you get this old.

When you were younger, your savings were more focused on the latest gadget, shoes, accessories, and fashion. You may not have saved to buy a home, car, or for your future wedding or in the event of sickness. The point is: it is never too early to start putting aside some of your income. Life is too unpredictable to not put some sort of financial preparation in place.

The penurial lifestyle is not attractive when you are single, and it will cause a strain on your union when you get married. One does not have to be rich, but the ability to help yourself is not in the least unattractive.

There is never a wrong time to save. Saving is preparation for the future. No one knows what the future entails, and that is exactly why you should put some of your earned income aside.

Tips on how to save:

- Make a budget: How much can you save each month without touching it?
- Open a savings account and have an automated system set up through the bank, where a sum is automatically withdrawn on a bi-weekly or monthly basis.
- Pay off outstanding debts, especially your credit card, quickly. Seek the assistance of a financial advisor so they can give you ideas or construct a financial plan as to how you can pay off what you owe in a timely fashion.
- Eat out less.
- Cut back on groceries.
- Pay attention to your spending.
- Cut back spending on things that will damage your health, like alcohol and cigarettes.

Benefits of saving:

- Helps in case of an emergency.
- A cushion to fall on if you lose your job.
- Helps for large purchases like a house or car without a loan.
- Leave a financial legacy for your family.
- Pay your own funeral costs.
- For retirement. Functions as a supplement to your pension.
- Helps to finance vacations.
- Helps to finance school fees for yourself or children.
- Helps finance your future wedding.

19
Treat Yourself, In Moderation

There is no shame in learning to take care of yourself. Some of us do an excellent job of taking care of others but not ourselves. While you are single, it is an excellent time to learn how to reward yourself in moderation. You do not have to receive praise or a gift from others after receiving that promotion or certificate; treat yourself, physically or verbally, if they did not.

If you work hard, then treat yourself to a spa treatment, facial, pedicure, manicure, trip, handbag, shoe, watch, wallet, or fashionable suit. Send yourself flowers on Valentine's Day. Appreciate yourself. What if you cannot afford to purchase an item? Then treat yourself verbally.

Self-Love Affirmations

1. I am fearfully and wonderfully made.
2. I am the apple of God's eyes.
3. **Ladies**: I am beautiful and gifted. **Gentlemen**: I am handsome and talented.
4. I deserve to be loved.
5. I am the perfect one for the right one.
6. I am deserving of all that is good.
7. I am of a sound mind.

8. I am at peace with myself.
9. I am seeking validation from no one but God.
10. I am resilient, strong, and determined.
11. I am excellence personified.
12. I am the epitome of success.
13. I am lovable.
14. I am wealthy with not just money but love and genuine friendships.
15. I am grateful and thankful.
16. I am experiencing God's favour in the land of the living.
17. I am creating a life that I am proud of.
18. I am leaving a great legacy for my child/ren.
19. I am making a positive impact on this earth.
20. I am my spouse's best friend, and our communication is excellent.
21. I am the answer to someone's prayer, so I am waiting on God's perfect timing.

Even when you do not work hard, pampering or treating yourself is nurturing to the mind. It uplifts the spirit and makes a bad day better. It makes a sad incident feel like one you will get over. Treating yourself will also make you more giving. What you like to do to relax may be what your spouse may also enjoy. It is a good thing to treat your spouse in moderation as well. Start practicing on yourself.

20
Meditate On Gods Promises

To meditate means to think over and over. It may also mean to deliberate over something repeatedly and bring it to the forefront of our thoughts for deep consideration and pondering upon deliberately.

Sometimes the negative gets trapped in our heads, and it is like a broken record that gets stuck on repeat. Often to cleanse our minds, bodies, and spirit, we need to focus on God's Word, His promises.

As mortal beings, when promises are made, there exists a possibility that such devoted words spoken may be broken. Such promises may be broken intentionally or unintentionally. However, God is not a man nor the son of a man that He should lie (See Numbers 23:19). There is only truth in Him, so while you wait to be wed, focus on repeating His many truthful, unfailing promises.

Here is a list of God's promises that you can focus on. There are others that you may read, research, and explore to find out.

Psalm 145:9
The Lord is good to all; he has compassion on all he has made. (NIV).

Psalm 84:11
For the Lord God is a sun and shield; the Lord bestows favour and honour; no good thing does he withhold from those who walk uprightly. (ESV).

Isaiah 40:29
He gives strength to the weary and increases the power of the weak. (NIV).

Deuteronomy 31:8
The LORD himself goes before you and will be with you; he will never leave you nor forsake you. Do not be afraid; do not be discouraged. (NIV).

Psalm 23:4
Even though I walk through the darkest valley, I will fear no evil, for you are with me; your rod and your staff, they comfort me. (ESV).

Matthew 6:31-33
So do not worry, saying, 'What shall we eat?' or 'What shall we drink?' or 'What shall we wear?' For the pagans run after all these things, and your heavenly Father knows that you need them. But seek first his kingdom and his righteousness, and all these things will be given to you as well. (NIV).

Proverbs 3:5-6
Trust in the Lord with all your heart and lean not on your own understanding; in all your ways submit to him, and he will make your paths straight. (NIV).

Psalm 34:10

The lions may grow weak and hungry, but those who seek the Lord lack no good thing. (NIV).

John 8:12

I am the light of the world. Whoever follows me will never walk in darkness, but will have the light of life. (ESV).

Psalm 37:4

Take delight in the Lord, and he will give you the desires of your heart. (NIV).

Philippians 4:7

And the peace of God, which surpasses every understanding, shall guard your hearts and your thoughts by Christ Jesus. (ESV).

Isaiah 40:31

But those who hope in the LORD will renew their strength. They will soar on wings like eagles; they will run and not grow weary, they will walk and not be faint. (NIV).

John 16:33

I have told you these things, so that in me you may have peace. In this world you will have trouble. But take heart! I have overcome the world. (NIV).

Jeremiah 31:3

I have loved you with an everlasting love; I have drawn you with unfailing kindness. (NIV).

John 15:9-10
As the Father has loved me, so have I loved you. Now remain in my love. If you keep my commands, you will remain in my love, just as I have kept my Father's commands and remain in his love. (NIV).

Psalm 121:5,7
The Lord watches over you—the Lord is your shade at your right hand... The Lord will keep you from all harm—he will watch over your life; the Lord will watch over your coming and going both now and forevermore. (NIV).

Remember, God is love, and He loves you unconditionally. Focus on the promises above and be encouraged; He wants you to have the best, including the best husband and wife that suits your personality and, most importantly, what you desire. Have confidence while you wait by meditating on His many promises.

21
Pray

If you desire to get married, please note God's Word instructs in Philippians 4:6: *"Do not be anxious about anything but in everything by prayer and supplication with thanksgiving let your requests be made known to God."* (ESV).

Mark 11:24 says: *"Therefore I tell you, whatever you ask for in prayer, believe that you have received it, and it will be yours."* (ESV).

Remember His Word in Proverbs 18:22: *"He who finds a wife finds a good thing and obtains favour from The Lord."* (NKJV).

Psalm 23:1 states: *"The Lord is my Shepherd, I lack nothing."* (NIV).

God designed marriage. He designed the beautiful intricacy and intimacy of a union that is intertwined with love for HIM first, then each other as man and woman; Adam, then Eve. The animals went in two by two in the ark. The sun by day and the moon by night. The heaven and the earth. The Lord saw the need for opposites functioning independently yet dependent on each other, thus complementing each other. The one who complements you is known by God, and when the time is right, he/she will be introduced to you by God. To everything there is a season under the sun, and the season will come in Jesus' name when you will be a wife or husband.

As you wait, here are some things to consider so your prayers can be specific as you pray for the kind of spouse you wish to be blessed with:

1. What are the qualities you desire in a spouse?

   _____
   _____
   _____
   _____

2. What kind of qualities do you NOT want your spouse to have?

   _____
   _____
   _____
   _____

3. What age group would you like your spouse to be? (If age matters to you).

   _____
   _____
   _____
   _____

4. Are there any specific physical traits that you like, or are you more concerned with the heart and/or character?

_____

_____

_____

_____

5. What kind of LOVE do you want to be blessed with?

_____

_____

_____

_____

6. What kind of parent do you want your spouse to be? (If you want or have a child or children).

_____

_____

_____

_____

7. Do you want to be married in three months, six months, or one year? When?

_____

_____

_____

_____

When we pray, let us ensure that we first BELIEVE. We believe in God and His Son, Jesus. Let us have NO DOUBT. Let us pray, thanking God in advance for our spouse because we have faith that it is already done. Pray, harboring no unforgiveness in your heart because we do not want anything to hinder us from praying with sincerity and love.

As you pray your specific prayers for a spouse, remember to pray that God removes qualities from your life that you know you need to work on to be a better version of yourself, so you are prepared emotionally, mentally and spiritually for who God has chosen for you.

God knows best, so your wife or husband may not come packaged as you wish, but God knows best. What you want in a spouse may not be what God knows you need for the marriage to last for eternity and not just for a season.

22
His And Hers Prayer Book And Journal

To help you on your journey of praying while you wait for your future spouse, I have compiled and completed a prayer book and journal that outlines specific characteristics and attributes that you may ask God that your future spouse possess.

The prayer book will come in two: one for women and another for men. It is a prayer companion, so there is an additional 21 MORE things to do while waiting for your future spouse. It is 21 specific prayers that you can pray every day until and even after you have met God's best for you. There is also a journal included for you to add your prayer points and requests for God to fulfill according to His will. This book will be available for sale very soon on some digital platforms.

I encourage both men and women to fast if they are desirous of marrying. I believe prayers are even more powerful and effective when fasting is accompanied. If you have never fasted before, here are some types of fasting that you can embark on. Choose the one that is manageable for you, and if you are a beginner, you will get stronger and can therefore go for longer periods without food or drink and perhaps even both. Please fast with caution. Exercise wisdom, especially if you have underlying health issues or you are pregnant. If you are hesitant to fast, go see your doctor before you begin any of the following.

Types of fasting according to the Bible:

1) The Samuel Fast (See 1 Samuel 7:6).
2) The Widow's Fast (See 1 Kings 17:16).
3) The Ezra Fast (See Ezra 8:23).
4) The Esther Fast (See Esther 4:16, 5:2).
5) The Elijah Fast (See 1 Kings 19:4,8).
6) The Daniel Fast (See Daniel 1:8).
7) The Disciple Fast (See Matthew 17:21 - KJV).
8) The Saint Paul Fast (See Acts 9:9).
9) The John the Baptist Fast (See Luke 1:15).
10) The Jesus Fast (See Matthew 4:2).

- For the Samuel Fast, no food or drink for one day or twenty-four hours.
- For the Esther Fast and Saint Paul Fast, there is no food or drink for three days.
- For the Jesus and Elijah Fast, there is no food or drink for forty days.
- For the Daniel Fast, only vegetables and water for ten days.
- For the John the Baptist Fast, abstain from wine or strong drink for one's entire life.

Each of the fast above was for a different purpose. You may choose to fast for your purpose. Aspire first to always draw closer to God during your time of fasting. It will happen naturally but seek Him first so that what you want will be given to you; even when you do not ask, the Lord, your God, knows what you need.

I usually break my fast with prayer or a Bible verse. I then bless the warm, not hot, beverage I will consume, followed by a light meal; small portions. In my early days of fasting, such restraint was not possible. I would eat like a farmer's horse at the end of a fasting period.

Please note, that although I have highlighted the Bible verse for each fast, I suggest reading the entire chapter to enhance your understanding.

Here are some links that will provide more information as it relates to the above mentioned scriptural fasting:

- https://www.gfc.cc/mt-content/uploads/2018/01/10-different-types-of-fasts-in-the-bible.pdf
- https://215ministry.com/10-proven-types-of-fasting-in-the-bible/

Singles, shift your perspective and see the power in waiting.

Unearth the possibilities of embarking upon self-discovery and preparing and being fully present and engaged in revealing and finding the man and woman God created you to be.

Pursue you and watch how the very best finds you.

Commit to finding you.

About The Author

Kadeen Dobbs' innate passion to write stems from a love of the Godhead. She is a teacher who has taught varying age groups across the educational spectrum and in different countries, from kindergarteners to adults. Kadeen also blogs. Her website is: http://kadeendobbs.wixsite.com/soaringtomynewbeginn. Her blogs explore and discuss a plethora of topics from a spiritual perspective.

Her intrinsic desire for imparting knowledge has transcended beyond the classroom and has prompted her to write a second book. Her first book is titled, *"Men And Women Of God Arise In The Workplace And Conquer! How To Navigate The Seas Of Jealousy, Envy And Sabotage."* In addition, her YouTube channel @Kadeen Dobbs has biblical affirmations to listen and declare that will uplift, encourage, empower and motivate men and women. Follow her on Instagram @ https://www.instagram.com/dobbskadeen/ for more inspiring content.

Notes

Notes

Notes

Notes

Notes